ACCOUNTING FOR SMALL BUSINESSES

QuickStart Guide

Understanding Accounting For Your Sole Proprietorship, Startup, & LLC

Edition # 1 – Updated : April 22, 2016

Cover Illustration and Design: Katie Poorman, Copyright © 2016 by ClydeBank Media LLC
Interior Design: Katie Poorman, Copyright © 2016 by ClydeBank Media LLC

ClydeBank Media LLC
P.O Box 6561
Albany, NY 12206
Printed in the United States of America

Copyright © 2016
ClydeBank Media LLC
www.clydebankmedia.com
All Rights Reserved

ISBN-13 : 978-1-945051-45-6

contents

INTRODUCTION 7

| 1 | THE IMPORTANCE OF GOOD ACCOUNTING 9

Taking Control of Your Cash Flow 9

Clear Profit/Loss Statements 9

Getting a Loan for Your Business 10

Preventing Fraud 10

| 2 | BALANCING YOUR CHECKBOOK 13

Reviewing Your Bank Statement 13

But What if it Doesn't? 15

| 3 | ACCOUNTING & YOUR BUSINESS ENTITY 17

| 4 | ASSETS, LIABILITIES, & EQUITY 21

Accrual Accounting vs. Cash Accounting 21

Assets 22

Liabilities 22

Equity 24

Double-Entry Accounting, Debits & Credits 27

Legend of Becky's Donut Shop 30

| 5 | RECORDING BUSINESS TRANSACTIONS 39

Source Documents 39

Chart of Accounts 40

Creating & Posting Journal Entries 42

Trial Balance 44

| 6 | FINANCIAL STATEMENTS 49

External & Internal Users 49

Types of Financial Statements 50

| 7 | BUDGETING FOR YOUR BUSINESS 55

    Why Budget? 56

    Budgeting Basics 57

    When Not to Budget 58

    Budgeting Software for Consideration 59

| 8 | FRAUD & ETHICS IN ACCOUNTING 61

| 9 | THE GAAP 67

    The Four Principles 68

    The Four Accounting Assumptions 70

| 10 | SIZING UP THE SOFTWARE 73

CONCLUSION 79

BONUS QUIZ 81

GLOSSARY 87

ABOUT CLYDEBANK 91

BEFORE YOU START READING, DOWNLOAD YOUR FREE DIGITAL ASSETS!

Visit the URL below to access your free Digital Asset files that are included with the purchase of this book.

☑ Summaries   ☑ White Papers
☑ Cheat Sheets   ☑ Charts & Graphs
☑ Articles   ☑ Reference Materials

DOWNLOAD YOURS HERE:

www.clydebankmedia.com/accounting-assets

introduction

Learning the fundamentals of accounting is like learning a new language. Becoming "literate" in accounting doesn't take quite as long as learning Russian, Spanish, or Chinese, but the advantages are indeed comparable.

It's safe to say that many people fear numbers – "I was terrible at math in school!" – so the word "accounting" calls up, for many, memories of days spent struggling over high school algebra. They prefer to leave the accounting to those who hang a CPA shingle outside their doors, confident that the professionals will do a much better job of managing their money.

But the fact remains that everyone should have a little accounting knowledge and, truly, the math involved isn't all that difficult. Nonetheless, knowing the basics, from how to balance your checkbook to learning to keep good financial records for tax purposes, goes a long way, whether you're a small business owner, investor, manager, lender, or just in charge of the household finances.

Having a clear knowledge of your business's financial life is important. No one should be in the dark about his or her overall financial picture. That's a disaster waiting to happen. However, with a perfunctory knowledge of basic accounting principles, including assets and liabilities, creating financial statements, budgeting, and more, you'll be on the road to a healthier relationship with your money.

| 1 |

The Importance of Good Accounting

There are a number of reasons to educate yourself on the particulars of accounting, some of them are quite basic but ultra-important.

Taking Control of Your Cash Flow

Small business owners tend to seek out help from accounting professionals when they notice that their businesses are having a difficult time managing cash flow, namely when they keep running out of cash, even though business seems to be moving along at a decent pace. Being able to model the business's financial activity using some basic accounting principles goes a long way toward identifying the source of the problems at hand and coming up with solutions.

Clear Profit/Loss Statements

If you're a small business owner with a lot of cash coming in and going out, then it can be difficult to figure out how much money you're actually making. Maybe you're considering buying a new house or car, or perhaps you've got a child headed to college. Fundamental accounting knowledge allows you to create clear profit-loss statements and to readily identify the value of your equity in your business. Furthermore, accounting literacy gives your business the power of financial forecasting, with which you can make optimal decisions to keep your business profitable.

Getting a Loan for Your Business

Maybe you've got a business model that's working well and you want to expand fast before swarms of copycats beat you to the punch. Or perhaps your business isn't doing so well financially, but you can make a pretty good case that a little capital support would quickly turn things around. Banks, lenders, and investors want to see properly-prepared financial statements before deciding whether or not to let you use their hard-earned money.

Preventing Fraud

Small businesses are at a bit of disadvantage when it comes to fraud prevention. To prevent fraud, larger companies often spread accounting responsibilities out over multiple parties and even departments. In small businesses, only one person often controls the books, and the business is forced to rely on both the integrity and competency of this person, who is often not even a professional accountant, but a bookkeeper (there's a big difference). If the owner or manager of the business has a fundamental understanding of accounting principles, then there's a much better chance for sound oversight and fraud prevention. Chapter 4 talks more about fraud.

One of the common misconceptions about accounting is that it's essentially the same thing as bookkeeping. In reality, accounting encompasses a much broader field of practice. Bookkeeping simply tracks the business's financial activities. It does not incorporate the critical analyses and specialized reporting that make accounting such a powerful resource for businesses of all sizes.

The accountant takes the numbers that the bookkeeper collects and translates them into a story, which he or she then relays to the business's decision-making executives. The accountant (usually acting in the capacity of a *CFO*) is responsible for discerning how these numbers have affected and will affect the business. Not to overly-dramatize an already terribly exciting profession, but if bookkeepers and accountants were likened to CIA surveillance operatives, then the bookkeepers would be responsible for setting up the surveillance equipment and recording and logging all of the incoming information, whereas the accountants would be in charge of discerning all actionable economic intelligence and reporting their findings in such a way that the special agents would know precisely where, when, and how to take action. Accountants are strategists, interpreters, and storytellers, responsible for relaying information from the world of numbers to the world of business.

| 2 |

Balancing Your Checkbook

Good accounting starts with the most basic of tasks, such as learning to properly balance your checkbook. This might seem like a given, but there are people (and businesses) who struggle with this each and every month and never seem to get it right. The result, unfortunately, is often a chronically unbalanced account that gets worse and worse each month. But it doesn't have to be that way if you invest a little time in this task.

Reviewing Your Bank Statement

So, your monthly bank statement has arrived and it's time to reconcile it. Here are a few simple steps to help you do this with ease:

Record Your Income & Transactions

Banks don't return canceled checks anymore, but they do provide digital images of those checks once they've cleared. Sit down with your statement and match each of those checks to the entries in your checkbook. Match check numbers as well as the amounts of the checks. Mark off each one you've matched. Note that when you pay bills electronically, banks do not include digital images of these e-checks along with your other checks

Verify Any Automatic Debits

Many people pay their insurance via a monthly withdrawal (debit) that's made by the vendor. Hopefully, you've allowed for these and have kept enough money in your account to cover them! Verify the amount deducted and where it was sent, just to be sure no changes were made since you first set up these payment plans.

Check Your Deposits

Hopefully, you've kept deposit receipts or have carefully entered them into your checkbook ledger. Check the amounts and dates. Remember, electronic deposits – perhaps paid to you by a customer or client – may take a few days to clear, so if they're made near the end of the month, they may appear on the next month's statement instead.

Look for any additional credits or debits including account service fees or interest. These small fees sometimes throw off your balance. When you've finished all of that, grab an old-fashioned pencil and a piece of paper and write down the balance that appears in your checkbook. Next,

- Deduct any authorized electronic debits.

- Add in any automatic payments you receive.

- Add up the uncleared checks (ones you haven't marked with a checkmark) and add that sum to your checkbook balance.

- Subtract any deposits that haven't yet cleared.

- Subtract any bank fees you've been charged.

- Add any interest paid.

- Add or subtract any recording errors you made as you were entering checks or deposits.

Voila! If you did it all correctly, your bank balance now matches the one on the statement you received from your financial institution.

But What if it Doesn't?

Usually, the frustration that builds at account balancing time generally comes down to finding the errors that cause YOUR balance to not match THEIR (the bank's) balance. Adding, subtracting... sometimes it seems as if you've done all the calculations a hundred times over but you still can't find the problem, but it needn't be that way.

Here are a few common reasons for a discrepancy:

Unrecorded Checks

First and foremost, the primary reason for differences in balance is unrecorded checks. These are checks that you wrote but forgot to record in your checkbook ledger or in the software program you use. This is where "duplicate" checks come in handy. Each one comes with a carbon copy that allows you to go back and see to whom you wrote that check, for how much, and when.

Outstanding Checks

You might also have outstanding checks. These are checks you've written or checks you've received that haven't yet cleared the bank.

Time

Differences can also be caused by deposits that have not yet been posted by the bank. If you deposited cash, it generally appears in your account immediately, but if the deposit was a check from another party and drawn on another bank, it might take a few days.

Automated Payments

Automated payments (deposits or withdrawals) are convenient, but they can sure mess up your accounting. We think nothing of sliding a card through a machine to make a purchase and often forget to record that transaction later. These mistakes cause many unbalanced checkbooks.

Interest

Interest earned adds a little to your account each month and might be the reason for that small discrepancy.

You Made a Mistake

Sometimes the problem just comes down to human error, usually on the part of the checking account owner. Double check your addition and subtraction if you've reviewed all of the above and still can't find the problem.

In the end, if you're still having problems, resist the urge to simply give up and record what the bank has said you have in your account. While the bank's accountin g is usually pretty solid, they do indeed make mistakes, and you may be doing yourself a disservice by simply taking their word for it. Keep at it a little longer and, if you still can't find the problem, call your bank and ask for assistance. Most of the time, they're eager to help.

Remember, keeping your checkbook balanced is important, mostly because it provides a quick overview of your business once a month. Those who ignore this task tend to get themselves into trouble, usually by spending more than is available. Get into the habit of balancing your account(s) no later than 24 hours after the statements arrive from the bank. You'll find that your peace of mind is well worth the small amount of time this task takes.

| 3 |

Accounting & Your Business Entity

No matter what kind of business you own, there IS accounting to take care of each month (or more often). However, if you're just getting started – or perhaps your business is still just a spark of an idea in your head – you need to make a choice about your business entity – that is, how you want to structure your business.

Your choices are as follows:

Sole Proprietorship
This type of business entity is the simplest to set up and the easiest to administer. This common form of business organization dictates that the owner is personally liable for all financial obligations associated with the business.

Partnership
As the name suggests, this entity involves two or more people who share in the profits and losses of the business. With a partnership, profits and losses are "passed through" to the partners to report on their own individual income tax returns. Hence, the individuals deal with profits and losses as a tax burden or advantage instead of the "partnership".

Corporations
Corporations are generally classified as "S" or "C". For small businesses, the S variety is the more common of the two options. C

Corporations tend to be for larger endeavors. With a corporation, the business entity is separate from the individual(s) who own it. In other words, when you choose corporate status you are avoiding personal legal liability. For many, that's the prime reason for selecting this entity. An S Corporation, on the other hand, allows you to avoid double taxation because you can – as with a partnership – "pass through" income and losses on individual tax returns.

Limited Liability Company (LLC)

Growing in popularity, the LLC allows owners to enjoy benefits of both a corporation and a partnership. Technically speaking, profits and losses can be passed through to the owners without taxation of the business itself, though owners are shielded from any liability. Many see it as a win-win situation.

Many issues influence how you choose from these entities. For instance, some are much easier to handle in regards to accounting and paperwork than others. Recordkeeping and accounting tend to be most complicated for those who choose corporations. Constant administrative matters take up lots of time and often prompt owners to hire accountants or other professionals rather than taking them on themselves. And that means more money spent and fewer profits.

Partnerships can involve complex accounting as well, simply because there are multiple owners involved in the business. It can get especially complicated at tax time when each partner must file his or her own Schedule K-1, which outlines his or her share of the losses, profits, and tax liabilities. That means ultra-careful accounting is necessary all year round so that tax documents are accurate when filed.

As far as ease of accounting is concerned, the sole proprietorship is by far the simplest. Mark Kalish, co-owner and vice president of EnviroTech Coating Systems Inc. in Eau Claire, Wisconsin, noted in a recent Entrepreneur Magazine article that he often chooses sole proprietorship because of the cost and time associated with bookkeeping and overall recordkeeping for the other types of entities.

> *"I would always take sole proprietorship as a first option,"* he says. *"If you're the sole proprietor and you own 100 percent of the business, and you're not in a business where a good umbrella insurance policy couldn't take care of potential liability problems, I would recommend a sole proprietorship. There's no real reason to encumber yourself with all the reporting requirements of a corporation unless you're benefiting from tax implications or protection from liability."*

However, if sole proprietorship is not the best choice for you, be prepared to learn how to do what it takes to keep your accounting up to date. Again, though it's easy just to turn it all over to an accountant, a business owner should always be familiar with the basic administrative needs of his company. If he is, he will always have access to a good overall look at how the company is faring and if any changes need to be made. If he's not, he's left in the dark.

| 4 |

Assets, Liabilities, & Equity

Accrual Accounting vs. Cash Accounting

While most small businesses tend to use a method known as *cash accounting*, *accrual accounting* is the accepted, standard method required by the Generally Accepted Accounting Principles (GAAP). We'll talk more about GAAP in Chapter 9.

The difference between the two methods is in how they define a formal transaction. In cash accounting, a transaction is the movement of money from one party to another. In accrual accounting, transactions are expressed in terms of accumulated assets and liabilities, which are two of the three main elements that create the *fundamental accounting formula*: *Assets = Liabilities + Equity*. Also known as the *accounting equation*, the fundamental accounting formula is an incredibly important concept in accounting, so much so that this chapter is entirely devoted to defining the component parts of this formula and explaining their applications.

So, here we are. Ground zero in the universe of accounting, the fundamental accounting formula:

$$Assets = Liabilities + Equity$$

Each of the three elements in this formula is a broad category that defines specific *accounts*.

Note : The technical definition of an "account" is a record of a particular type of expenditure, arrearage, obligation, or revenue collection opportunity. Every different "account" is classified as an asset, liability, equity, revenue, or expense.

Assets

An asset can be cash held in a checking account (or under your mattress). An asset can also be an AR (accounts receivable) account—a record of what someone else owes your business. Asset accounts also include "physical" items you own such as equipment, real estate, land, or supplies.

Think of asset accounts as *forward leaning* accounts, meaning that they indicate potential money that, theoretically, will be coming into your business at some point. It gets a little confusing here, since assets can also include cash because cash is a promise of incoming value, guaranteed by the government which printed/issued it.

Think of other assets in the same way. If you have a $10,000 piece of farm machinery, a nice tractor perhaps, then that tractor presumably promises to offer a great deal of real value to your business. Or, if it doesn't, then you can always convert the tractor into cash (sell it) so as to promise value for your business in some other way. The tractor, just like the cash, is an asset: a promise of value to your business.

Other common examples of a business entity's assets include the business's product inventory and the business's investments, both of which, true to form, represent a promise of future value.

Liabilities

Liabilities represent value scheduled to depart the business. An example of a liability account includes AP (*accounts payable*) - money that you owe to another business or individual. Liabilities also include *notes payable* accounts, which are debts that your business is paying back to banks or other lenders (both short- and long-term debts). Liabilities include "unearned revenue" accounts, or services for which the business has already been paid but has yet to perform. For example, if a famous pop singer has been given a hundred thousand dollars to make a special guest appearance on a television show, that hundred thousand dollars constitutes a liability for the pop singer if the television show pays the pop singer *before* she shows up to do the appearance. Even though she will incur an asset (presumably $100,000 in cash), she also has a $100,000 liability until the work is performed.

*Example : Just in case you find yourself thinking a little too much about this (you don't need to at this point), here's what technically happens with the pop singer's TV deal in terms of the fundamental accounting formula. After the deal is made and she gets paid, her accountant records the $100,000 in a distinct "prepaid cash __asset__ account." The accountant also records the $100,000 as an obligation in an "unearned revenue __liability__ account." Once the pop singer makes the TV appearance, fulfilling her obligation, her accountant reduces (or **debits**) her unearned revenue liability account by $100,000, while crediting $100,000 to her normal revenue account, which is technically an equity account. Meanwhile, the accountant also needs to move the $100,000 out of the prepaid cash asset account into a normal cash asset account. This is also done in two strokes with a specific debit and a **credit**. Debiting and crediting will be covered later on in this chapter in a discussion of the fundamentals of **double-entry accounting**.*

note	date	account	Assets	=	account	Liabilities	+	account	Equity
TV deal is made	5/1/2015	prepaid cash	$100,000.00		unearned revenue	$100,000.00		revenue	$ -
		regular cash	$ -						
Pop Singer Appears on show	6/15/2015	prepaid cash	$ -		unearned revenue	$ -		revenue	$100,000.00
		regular cash	$100,000.00						

Fg. 1

*Now, what do you notice about the 5/1/15 and the 6/15/15 snapshots of the pop star's account in **Fg.1**? If you're brand new to accounting, then the only thing that you really need to understand is that in both snapshots, the pop singer's total assets always equal the sum of her liabilities and her equity (if the pop singer is a business entity). On 5/1/15 she has $100,000 in* *total assets, $100,000 in liabilities and no money in equity. On 6/15/15, she has $100K in assets, $0 liabilities and $100K in equity. The fundamental accounting formula (Assets = Liabilities + Equity) must always hold true. If you're already feeling a little overwhelmed, don't panic. Getting your head around the fundamentals of accounting involves pushing through certain periods of study in which your understanding is limited to bits and pieces. Think of learning accounting as similar to watching a Polaroid photograph develop. It's gradually going to take shape and come into focus. You must give it time.*

Equity

If you read just the fundamental accounting formula, you get:

$$Assets - Liabilities = Equity$$

And that's more or less exactly what equity is: the assets left over after a company's liabilities have all been accounted for—otherwise known as net assets. Remember, when you use the fundamental accounting formula, you're applying it on behalf of a business entity. The formula simplifies what can often be a very complex financial ecosystem, with many moving parts (payroll, overhead, debt, sales, office supplies, cost of goods sold, equipment, and on and on). Think about it: once a business entity has assets equal to its liabilities, then that business, as an entity unto itself, is financially solvent. So anything left over, the excess of the assets after all liabilities are clear, must end up somewhere. Usually, this "equity" goes to the owner, the shareholders, or back into the operations of the business.

The four most common types of equity accounts are:

1. **Owners' Capital** : This account keeps track of all money that the owner(s) put into the business.

2. **Owner Withdrawals** : This account keeps track of all the money that the owner(s) take out of the business.

3. **Revenues** : Also known as "sales," the revenues account tracks the gross increase in equity that transpires when the company takes in money.

4. **Expenses** : Expense accounts track the use of assets (such as the checking account) in the pursuit of additional revenues. Examples include utilities, insurance, supply costs, and employee costs.

Given these four fundamental types of equity, the fundamental accounting formula can be expanded to:

$$\text{Assets} = \text{Liabilities} + (\text{Owner Capital} - \text{Owner Withdrawals} + \text{Revenues} - \text{Expenses})$$

To help you understand how it all fits together, consider the following practice problem:

After its first full fiscal year is in the books, Jack's Plumbing has recorded $575,000 in revenue and $80,000 in expenses. The company's current assets have a combined value of $800,000. The company's owner, Jack Mayfield, used $100,000 of his own money to start the company and has withdrawn $60,000 over the course of the fiscal year.

What is the total value of the liabilities held by Jack's Plumbing?

To solve this problem, take a look at the expanded version of the fundamental accounting formula.

$$\text{Assets} = \text{Liabilities} + (\text{Owner Capital} - \text{Owner Withdrawals} + \text{Revenues} - \text{Expenses})$$

You know the total amount of the company's assets ($800,000), and you can calculate equity by subtracting owner withdrawals ($60,000) from owner capital ($100,000) and adding the total ($40,000) to the difference of the company's revenues ($575,000) minus the company's expenses ($80,000). To calculate total equity, you add $40,000 to $495,000 to get $535,000.

$$\$800,000 = ? + (\$100,000 - \$60,000 + \$575,000 - \$80,000)$$

Going back to the simplified version of the formula:

$$\$800,000 \text{ (assets)} = \text{(liabilities)} + \$535,000 \text{ (equity)}$$

By subtracting the company's equity from its total assets, you can deduce that Jack's Plumbing should hold a total of $265,000 in liabilities if all the other numbers are indeed accurate.

In the real world Jack would have records (accounts) for all of his liabilities, presumably records that totaled to $265,000. If the liabilities recorded did not total to $265,000, then there would be a discrepancy somewhere in the books, and it would need to be resolved through research. That's accounting.

> *Note : In case you're wondering, you can't (except by some rare, complicated, and mostly irrelevant exceptions) have a negative asset balance or a negative liability balance. To get your equity, the liabilities held are essentially weighed against the assets held. If there are more liabilities than assets, however, then you can certainly have a negative equity, also known as a "debit" equity balance. Debits and credits are covered later in this chapter and may require some extra study.*

Double-Entry Accounting, Debits & Credits

The concept of ***double-entry accounting*** is at the core of accounting methodology. Double-entry accounting assures that your assets always equal your liabilities plus your equity. Though accountants still use double-entry accounting religiously today, the concept itself dates back to the 15th century. Luca Pacioli was an Italian Franciscan monk who is, to use some accountant humor, *credited* with inventing debits and credits to track complex accounts.

Now, you may, as most non-accountants do, think of debits and credits as relatively simple concepts: debits occur when money is taken away, and credits occur when money comes in. In accounting, it's not quite so simple. In double-entry accounting, every transaction made, whether internally or externally, must be noted by an account credit and by a corresponding debit of the same amount, but in a different account.

Here are some examples to help you get a foothold on double-entry accounting while also explaining the difference between an external and ***internal transaction***. An ***external transaction*** occurs when Tony's Pizza Parlor pays The Weekly Deal to put a Tony's Pizza Parlor coupon sheet in their coupon circular. It's an advertising expense. Assume Tony pays The Weekly Deal in cash. The transaction would be noted thus:

1. A credit in the Tony's Pizza Parlor's cash account. (Yes, it is a "credit," even though cash is leaving. Just go with it for now.) A cash account, as you should know by now, is an "asset," so is a checking account, savings account, or a stock portfolio. The nice thing about assets is that they're intuitive—if it sounds like an asset, then it probably is an asset.

2. A debit to Tony's Pizza Parlor's expense account, which, as you should know by now, is an equity account.

An internal transaction occurs when account value is transferred within a business without affecting any outside entities. For example, Tony has a valuable signed photograph of Joe DiMaggio that's worth an estimated $50,000, and because it's so valuable, it's considered a company asset. One day, out of nowhere the photograph goes missing and no one has any clue where it went. It's assumed that the photograph was stolen. Since the photograph is considered a company asset, its loss is noted using the following transactions:

1. A credit (yes, a credit) is entered in Tony's Pizza Parlor's interior decorations (asset) account for $50,000.

2. A debit is recorded in Tony's Pizza Parlor's expense (equity) account.

A lot of people find that when learning how to properly distinguish between debits and credits, it's best to think in terms of left and right.

Let's look again at the fundamental accounting formula:

Assets = Liabilities + Equity

Assets are on the left of the equation, liabilities and equity on the right. Now, think of it this way: when someone at the supermarket takes your card for payment, they often ask you this question:

"Debit or Credit?"

For the purpose of this lesson, think of debit as always being on the left and credit as always being on the right.

When dealing with assets (left), when a transaction increases your business's assets, it is said to *debit* the assets. When a transaction decreases your assets, it's said to credit your assets. Counterintuitive, sure, but ultimately necessary to form an airtight system whereby every transaction that your business makes may always be traced back to both a credit and a debit.

> *Note : In other words, if a satisfied customer writes your business a fat check because your team did a bang-up job, there still must be some "debit" that gets associated with that transaction. In this case, your company's revenue (equity) account would receive a credit and your company's checking account would receive—purely for accounting purposes—a debit. Is it beginning to make sense?*

When dealing with liabilities (right), a debit always decreases the liability and a credit increases it. Also counterintuitive, but mathematically practical. So, every month when your small business pays $2,500 toward its bank note, the bank note (liability) account is debited by $2,500, while the checking account (asset) that you used to make your payment is credited—for accounting purposes—$2,500, even though your checking account balance actually went down.

Think of it this way: the normal situation in a business is a steady accumulation of assets. You purchase equipment, your checking account balances go up so you purchase some office space. These increases in your assets are normal, and they are all considered debits. Debits are always on the left, and assets are always on the left. Debits are "normal."

Liabilities are on the right, as are credits. It's normal for a business to incur liabilities. So long as the business needs to order more and more new products, the accounts payable (AP) liability account continues to increase. When customers make deposits (before goods have been shipped) the "customer deposits" liability account increases. Payable taxes are also a liability that should continually increase during the normal course of business. So, think of liabilities being on the right and credits being on the right as a way to remember that credits always increase liabilities. Debits, by contrast, decrease liabilities.

Like liabilities, equity is also on the right. Under normal business conditions, equity (hopefully) increase, therefore increases to equity are denoted by credits and decreases by debits.

If you're still not clear on how everything fits together, or if you're beginning to become clear but would just like an added refresher, here's a story (or "summary") of simple accounting transactions that use debits, credits, and the fundamental accounting formula.

The Legend of Becky's Donut Shop

A tale told in the language of accounting

Chapter 1 : The Owner Invests

Becky has worked hard and has saved up enough money to open up her very own donut shop in downtown Louisville, Kentucky. To get started, she's going to put $250,000 of her own money into this investment.

Assets	=		Liabilities	+		Equity
cash			$ -			Owner's Capital
$250,000.00			$ -			

Fg. 2

Since Becky invested 250K of her own money into the donut shop, she's increased her equity in the business. Since you've been hired to be Becky's accountant, you are going to enter a $250,000 credit in the owner's capital equity account. All equity accounts are on the right, and therefore, credits are used to describe increases in equity accounts. On the left side, you now have $250,000 in cash in your cash assets account. Since all assets are on the left, you're going to *debit* the account to signify the increase in assets.

Chapter 2 : The Territory is Secured

Becky is going to pay a deposit on her first month's rent on the small building that's she's using for her donut shop. The building is right next to a major grocery store, so it will certainly enjoy a lot of visibility. The owner of the building requires a $3,000 deposit and $1,500 for the first month's rent, a total expense of $4,500.

		Assets	=	Liabilities	+			Equity
		cash		$ -				Owner's Capital
(1)		$ 250,000.00		$ -				$ 250,000.00
(2)		cash		$ -		Expense		Owner's Capital
		$ 250,000.00		$ -			$ (4,500.00)	$ 250,000.00
		$ (4,500.00)						
	Total Assets					Total Equity		
	$ 245,500.00					$ 245,500.00		

Fg. 3

In chapter 2 of this legend, Becky paid her deposit and first month's rent for her building. This transaction is shown by a debit (decrease) in the expense equity account and a credit (decrease) in the cash account, both decreases in the amount of $4,500.

Chapter 3 : The Tools are Gathered

In this chapter, Becky purchases the equipment she needs to make the donuts at her store. She purchases the equipment with cash, and her total expenditure is $25,000.

Notice in *Fg. 4* that the cash account was credited with 25,000 to purchase equipment. A new asset account called "equipment" was created, and it was debited in the amount of $25,000 to indicate that the business now holds $25,000 worth of assets in the form of donut shop equipment. Notice that Becky's total assets still equal $245,500 (the sum of the new cash balance and the value of the equipment). As always, assets are equal to liabilities and equity.

	Assets		=	Liabilities	+		Equity
(2)	cash			$ -		Expense	Owner's Capital
	$ 250,000.00			$ -		$ (4,500.00)	$ 250,000.00
	$ (4,500.00)						
	Total Assets					Total Equity	
	$ 245,500.00					$ 245,500.00	
(3)	Cash	Equipment		$ -		Expense	Owner's Capital
	$ 250,000.00	$ 25,000.00		$ -		$ (4,500.00)	$ 250,000.00
	$ (4,500.00)						
	$ (25,000.00)						
new cash balance	$ 220,500.00						
	Total Assets					Total Equity	
	$ 245,500.00					$ 245,500.00	

Fg. 4

Chapter 4 : Donuts Don't Make Themselves

Becky now has the equipment and the space she needs to make donuts. But in order to make donuts, you also need dough, filling, powdered sugar, and much more. These supplies will be coming in on a regular basis. Becky hopes to find a good wholesale vendor, and she finds one in Maverick's Food Supply. Maverick's has all the supplies she needs, everything from dough to napkins. Becky places her first order with Maverick's in the amount of $750. Maverick's fulfills the order on credit, and Becky won't have to pay until the end of the month.

	Assets		=	Liabilities	+		Equity
(3)	Cash	Equipment		$ -		Expense	Owner's Capital
	$ 250,000.00	$ 25,000.00		$ -		$ (4,500.00)	$ 250,000.00
	$ (4,500.00)						
	$ (25,000.00)						
new cash balance	$ 220,500.00						
	Total Assets					Total Equity	
	$ 245,500.00					$ 245,500.00	
(4)	Cash	Equipment		AR (Mavericks)		Expense	Owner's Capital
	$ 250,000.00	$ 25,000.00		$ 750.00		$ (4,500.00)	$ 250,000.00
	$ (4,500.00)					$ (750.00)	
	$ (25,000.00)						
new cash balance	$ 220,500.00						
	Total Assets			Total Liabilities		Total Equity	
	$ 245,500.00			$ 750.00		$ 244,750.00	

Fg. 5

Maverick's is an AP or ***Accounts Payable*** account. AP simply refers to any account where another business or person has provided goods or services for which you've yet to pay. All AP accounts are liabilities, as they indicate a future obligation. Though the raw material needed to make donuts technically falls under the category of ***COG or Cost of Goods Sold***, for now you're just going to treat all of the goodies that Maverick's is sending to Becky as "supplies," and debit your expense account accordingly in the amount of $750.00. Notice that Becky's total assets remain equal to her total liabilities plus total equity.

Chapter 5 : Finding the Right Help & Opening for Business

Becky anticipates that when she first opens up she will be met by a rush of customers wanting to try out the new donut shop. Therefore, she decides to hire two employees before opening day. After the first week, Becky's Donut Shop has brought in $4,235 in sales. Her two employees have worked a combined 63 hours, and she's agreed to pay them both $10/hr, though paychecks won't go out until the end of week two.

		Assets	=	Liabilities		+		Equity	
(4)	Cash	Equipment		AP (Mavericks)			Expense	Owner's Capital	
	$ 250,000.00	$ 25,000.00		$ 750.00			$ (4,500.00)	$ 250,000.00	
	$ (4,500.00)						$ (750.00)		
	$ (25,000.00)								
new cash balance	$ 220,500.00								
	Total Assets			Total Liabilities			Total Equity		
	$ 245,500.00			$ 750.00			$ 244,750.00		
(5)	Cash	Equipment		AP (Mavericks)	Accrued Payroll		Expense	Revenue	Owner's Capital
	$ 250,000.00	$ 25,000.00		$ 750.00	$ 630.00		$ (4,500.00)	$ 4,235.00	$ 250,000.00
	$ (4,500.00)						$ (750.00)		
	$ (25,000.00)						$ (630.00)		
	$ 4,235.00								
new cash balance	$ (224,735.00)								
	Total Assets			Total Liabilities			Total Equity		
	$ 249,735.00			$ 1,380.00			$ 248,355.00		

Fg. 6

As you can see in *Fg. 6,* the revenue collected from the week is recorded both in the revenue equity account and the cash asset account. When you (Becky's accountant) help Becky assess her finances at the end of her first week of business, you'll presumably have all of the cash from her revenue on-hand and will be able to immediately deposit it into her bank account, or wherever she's storing her cash assets. With payroll, however, though you've recorded the liability and the expense, it does not impact your cash supply at this time, because employees won't be paid until the following week. However, since the services have already been rendered, the obligation becomes what's known as an *accrued liability*, and must be debited out of your equity. As you may have noticed, in this chapter you've actually covered two separate transaction records: the collection of revenue and a record of accrued employee payroll liability.

Chapter 6 : Time to Pay the Piper

At the end of week two, a lot of things happen in Becky's Donuts. Her employees have not only earned another week of wages, but need to be paid. Becky wants her pay periods set up so that employees are paid for the immediately preceding weeks, so she has two weeks of payroll cost leaving the business. During week two, Becky's Donut Shop brought in $4,516 in revenue. The business's two employees worked for a combined 59 hours at a rate of $10/hr. The Maverick's AR account won't need to be paid until the end of the month, but she's nearly out of supplies, so she orders another $750 worth of goods from Maverick's. Finally, Becky's dear 15-year-old cat requires a very expensive surgical procedure, and she's made the decision to take $3,200 in cash out of the business in order to pay the veterinarian.

Becky's given you a lot to keep track of here. Hopefully, she's paying you well. Accountants, though, just like everyone else, are subject to making mistakes. One of the things that makes accounting really useful, however, is the methodology used to get to the bottom of any errors, whether they were your errors or errors made by someone else in the company. Consider the following summary for Chapter 6:

	Assets		=	Liabilities		+			Equity	
(5) Cash		Equipment		AP (Mavericks)	Accrued Payroll		Expense	Revenue	Owner's Capital	
	$ 250,000.00	$ 25,000.00		$ 750.00	$ 630.00		$ (4,500.00)	$ 4,235.00	$ 250,000.00	
	$ (4,500.00)						$ (750.00)			
	$ (25,000.00)						$ (630.00)			
	$ 4,235.00									
new cash balance	$ 224,735.00									
	Total Assets			Total Liabilities			Total Equity			
	$ 249,735.00			$ 1,380.00			$ 248,355.00			
(6) Cash		Equipment		AP (Mavericks)	Accrued Payroll		Expense	Revenue	Owner's Capital	Owner Withdrawl
	$ 250,000.00			$ 750.00	$ 630.00		$ (4,500.00)	$ 4,235.00	$ 250,000.00	$ (3,200.00)
	$ (4,500.00)			$ 750.00	($ 630.00)		$ (750.00)	$ 4,516.00		
	$ (25,000.00)						$ (630.00)			
	$ 4,235.00						$ (590.00)			
this week's payroll	$ (590.00)						$ (750.00)			
last week's payroll	$ (630.00)									
owner withdrawl	$ (3,200.00)									
new cash balance	$ 220,315.00									
	Total Assets			Total Liabilities			Total Equity			
	$ 245,315.00			$ 1,500.00			$ 248,331.00			

Fg. 7

You can always check the accuracy of the statement by looking at those bottom lines. Do total assets equal liabilities plus equity? In *Fg. 7* your assets total to $245,315, while your liabilities and equity sum up to $249,831. You must have missed something. Take a moment and see if you can figure out what you missed before Becky fires you. To make things a little easier, list all entries pertaining to new transactions for Chapter 6. After all, if you look back to the Chapter 5 transactions you'll see that your equation was balanced. The error must therefore be in Chapter 6. Your Chapter 6 "week two" events include:

- $4,516 in additional revenue/sales – (Becky's got great donuts!)
- Employees earned $590 this week and you paid it straight out of your cash account.
- Becky's employees' earnings from last week (accrued payroll) was paid out in cash to the tune of $630.
- The company owner, Becky, took out $3,200 to pay for her cat's surgery.
- Another order was placed with Maverick's in the amount of $750 for more supplies.

Have you found the error yet?

If not, here's a hint – and generally a good way to solve accounting errors—figure out the amount by which your fundamental accounting formula is out of balance. According to *Fg. 7*, you have a total of $245,315 in total assets and $249,831 in equity plus liabilities, a difference of $4,516. What you'll usually find in accounting is that these differences are not random numbers, but clues that help you find the problem. Does the number $4,516 show up anywhere else?

Did you find it yet? It's your total sales from week two. In *Fg. 7* you've recorded (credited) the revenue but neglected to make a debit elsewhere. Remember, every transaction must always include both a credit and a debit. That's the genius of double-entry accounting. Ok, so, since your revenue for last week entails cash-in-hand, you need to "debit" your cash account, which adds $4,516 to your total assets and balances the formula.

In the real world an error such as this one may indicate that someone didn't make a deposit per schedule. This could even indicate that someone took cash home without authorization. The source for the revenue report may be the register, which, in your example would show $4,516 in sales. As Becky's accountant, you need to be able to pinpoint exactly where and when this money went missing. You should be able to tell the client (Becky) who was working on the day the cash went missing and who was responsible for depositing the cash in the bank, safe or elsewhere. Fraud will come up in Chapter 8. For now, just assume that the cash was found and that the error was on your part, forgetting to do the second half of the double-entry procedure. You can view the correct record in *Fg. 8* on the following page.

You've corrected the record by adding a debit to your cash account to offset the credit you entered into your revenue account. Your assets are again equal to your liabilities plus equity, and all is right with the world.

	Assets		=	Liabilities		+		Equity		
(6)	Cash	Equipment		AP (Mavericks)	Accrued Payroll		Expense	Revenue	Owner's Capital	Owner Withdrawl
	$ 250,000.00	$ (25,000.00)		$ 750.00	$ 630.00		$ (4,500.00)	$ (4,235.00)	$ 250,000.00	$ (3,200).00
	$ (4,500.00)			$ 750.00	($ 630.00)		$ (750.00)	$ (4,516.00)		
	$ (25,000.00)						$ (630.00)			
last week's sales	$ 4,235.00						$ (590.00)			
this week's payroll	$ (590.00)						$ (750.00)			
last week's payroll	$ (630.00)									
this week's sales	$ 4,516.00									
owner withdrawl	$ (3,200.00)									
new cash balance	$ 224,831.00									
	Total Assets			Total Liabilities			Total Equity			
	$ 249,831.00			$ 1,500.00			$ 248,331.00			

Fg. 8

Hopefully, you've enjoyed the Legend of Becky's Donuts, a story told in the language of accounting. It's important to understand that the images used in this story aren't formatted in the way that real accounting records would be formatted. For starters, transactions are usually dated or organized by number (not organized by chapter). Using dates to sequence the financial snapshots allows owners, managers, and other stakeholders to follow the financial timeline of the business. The main purpose of the Becky's Donuts example was just to help you drill your understanding of the mechanics involved in double-entry accounting and the use of "credits" and "debits." The following chapters focus more on the proper presentation of accounting information.

| 5 |

Recording Business Transactions

Once you understand the fundamental accounting formula, you've got most of the mathematical complexities covered. As strange as it may seem, accounting doesn't really involve a lot of difficult math, really just addition and subtraction. The challenge is learning how to keep the basic math organized properly so that it's truly useful, even indispensable, to the business. That's really what makes an accountant special, not the ability to compute. Any software program can compute—heck, any calculator can do the same. It's the ability to translate the numbers into a story that shines light on the direction and needs of the business.

Note : In the back of this book (pg. xx) there's a quiz to help you practice identifying various types of accounts.

In order to maximize their utility to the business, accountants use specific methods and tools to keep all the numbers in order. This chapter reviews a few of these most fundamental methods and tools. If you're a small business owner, then rest assured that by the end of this chapter you'll understand what your accountant means when he says he needs to make a *journal entry* or when he gives you a *trial balance*. Or, if you're planning on doing your business's accounting on your own, then this chapter will teach you to apply these powerful concepts.

Source Documents

Source documents inform the changes in value of various accounts. Examples of source documents include: bills from service providers, sales slips and reports indicating that the business took in revenue, and records on employee earnings. Bank statements are also used as source documents to determine changes that must be made to various accounts within the business.

Chart of Accounts

A *chart of accounts* is a list of all accounts within the umbrella of assets, liabilities, and equity.

If you're operating a small business, then you may have as few as twenty or thirty different accounts to manage, whereas large companies may have several thousand accounts. Even small businesses fare better if they number their accounts in an organized fashion. An effective, expandable filing system should have a structure that looks something like this:

- 101-199   Asset accounts
- 201-299   Liability accounts
- 301-399   Equity accounts
- 401-499   Revenue accounts
- 501-599   Expense accounts

As you can see, there are about 100 available account types for each big-bucket category. Most small businesses never require more than these. The first digit in the three-number sequence identifies the big-bucket account type, asset, liability, etc., while the second two digits can further categorize accounts. For example, every account beginning with a 10 (101, 102, 103...) may be a type of cash account, including checking accounts, savings accounts, petty cash, cash equivalents, accounts receivable, or office supplies. Every asset account beginning with 11 (110, 111, 112...) may represent various product inventory accounts. Once you get to the 200s, you're dealing entirely with liability accounts, which may also be broken up into their own various subcategories: short-term liabilities, long-term liabilities, tax liabilities, debts and so forth for each account family.

If your small business has multiple owners, then you can use the chart of accounts numbering system to keep track of each owner's distinct asset account. For example, imagine you run a modeling and talent agency and there are three principal owners, Larry, Curly, and Moe. Your equity accounts may be:

- 301   Larry, Owner's Capital
- 302   Larry, Owner's Withdrawal
- 303   Curly, Owner's Capital
- 304   Curly, Owner's Withdrawal
- 305   Moe, Owner's Capital
- 306   Moe, Owner's Withdrawal

Use a chart of accounts to think about and organize all your business's account types before you start building your physical filing system.

Note : Even though you can do a lot of accounting on the computer, you still need a basic accounting filing system in which you keep physical receipts and other accounting paperwork. This doesn't have to mean clutter. In fact, many small businesses can get away with having one cabinet each for assets, liabilities, and equity. You may want to begin with the equity cabinet divided into two cabinets, one for revenue and expenses, and the other for owner's capital and owner's withdrawals. That's just four filing cabinets required to get your small business financially organized. Not bad at all!

The types of accounts that you find in your chart of accounts vary significantly based on the type of industry. If your small business were a physician's group, then you'd have very different account types than you'd have if you were a construction business.

Note : In addition to "Chart of Accounts," you're also likely to hear the term general ledger to describe a complete listing of all the accounts a business uses. There isn't really any substantial difference between these two terms, but, technically speaking, the Chart of Accounts must include the assigned account number next to each account, whereas a ledger simply means a listing, numbered or unnumbered. In *addition to the general ledger, there are also account-specific **ledgers**, which track the activity (debits and credits) of a specific account. These single account ledgers are, in fact, very important to the next section in this chapter.*

Creating & Posting Journal Entries

Journal entries are used to keep a record of every transaction relevant to a business's accounting. Journal entries utilize source documents to identify relevant transaction components. A credit and a debit must always be recorded on a journal entry, and, once complete, the entry is posted in a general journal—which every company should have—and any specialized journals that the company wishes to maintain. Journal entries must always have the following four components:

- The date of the transaction including day, month, and year.
- The names and numbers—per the chart of accounts—of the accounts that were debited.
- The names and numbers of the accounts that were credited.
- A short explanation of the transaction, such as: "purchase of a new steamer for restaurant."

When it comes to formatting, so long as you have the four points of information specified above, then you can format your journal entries as you please. It's typical to offset the name of the account (usually by indenting it to the left) to separate it from the rest of the information about the transaction. It's also customary to leave a blank line between each journal entry to keep each entry visually distinct.

Posting is the process of moving information in the journal to the general ledger for each account affected. Consider the following example:

Margaret owns a beauty salon, and she or her accountant makes a journal entry to document that the 101 cash account is credited by $2,500 to pay for a new hair dryer chair. On that same journal entry, the $2,500 is debited on the 165 store equipment account. The entry is dated and a note is made, "purchased new dryer chair." At some point that journal information needs to be added to the respective ledgers for both the 101 cash account and the 165 store equipment account. The process of moving this information from the journal to the general ledgers is known as posting. Posting is completed in four steps:

Step One

Locate the ledger for the debit account. (In the case of the example above, Margaret should find her 165 store equipment account ledger in her assets filing cabinet.) Enter the date of the transaction into the 165 ledger. The page of the journal should be recorded as well in the Posting Reference column (PR column) in the ledger.

Step Two

Record the amount of the debit and the remaining balance of the account.

Step Three

Next, the debit account number (165 in this example) must be entered into the PR column of the journal.

Then identify the credit account from the journal entry (in this example the account is Margaret's 101 cash account), and retrieve the ledger. In the ledger write the date, the journal page, the amount credited, and record the new balance.

Step Four

Finally, the credit account number (101 in this example) must be recorded in the PR column of the journal.

And voila! Your posting is complete!

The purpose of posting journal entries is to leave a thorough financial trail of well-connected records. When discrepancies arise, it is easier to trace them back to the source when your business's journals and ledgers are well maintained.

Trial Balance

A trial balance is a common way to check for accuracy in your accounts. In it, you list the balances of all accounts your business maintains and verify that the total of all the debit balances are equal to the total of all the credit balances.

> *Note : What constitutes a debit or credit balance depends on the type of account. Asset accounts usually have a debit balance, meaning that there is indeed some cash-on-hand, some cash in your checking account, and your equipment has some value (as opposed to negative value). Liabilities and equity accounts, in their normal state, should have a credit balance, meaning that you do indeed owe money to your credit card companies, you do have revenue, and you do have some owner capital tied up in the business. Debit balances in liability and equity accounts are not normal.*

Trial Balance XYZ Trading as at 30 June 2010		
General Ledger Accounts	(Dr. - Debit)	(Cr. - Credit)
Cash at bank	10,000	
Inventory	40,000	
Vehicles	30,000	
Fixtures & Fittings	32,000	
Accounts Receivable	15,000	
Credit Cards Payable		12,000
Accounts Payable		15,000
Bank Loan		50,000
Sales		175,000
Purchases	60,000	
Advertising	5,000	
Wages	65,000	
Rent	15,000	
Electricity	5,000	
Owners Capital		25,000
TOTAL	277,000	277,000

Fg. 9

Here's an example of what a trial balance sheet looks like:

Notice that the total of all debit balances ($277,000) is equal to the total of all credit balances (also $277,000). The number $277,000 has no real relevance in and of itself; it's just a measurement of the balance held between the accounts in the business.

As an exercise, take a few minutes to come up with your own trial balance using the account information from Becky's Donut Shop (see Chapter 1). Here's a snapshot of the donut shop's most recent accounts:

	Assets		=	Liabilities		+	Equity			
(6)	Cash	Equipment		AP (Mavericks)	Accrued Payroll		Expense	Revenue	Owner's Capital	Owner Withdrawl
	$ 250,000.00	$ (25,000.00)		$ 750.00	$ 630.00		$ (4,500.00)	$ (4,235.00)	$ 250,000.00	$ (3,200.00)
	$ (4,500.00)			$ 750.00	($ 630.00)		$ (750.00)	$ (4,516.00)		
	$ (25,000.00)						$ (630.00)			
last week's sales	$ 4,235.00						$ (590.00)			
this week's payroll	$ (590.00)						$ (750.00)			
last week's payroll	$ (630.00)									
this week's sales	$ 4,516.00									
owner withdrawl	$ (3,200.00)									
new cash balance	$ 224,831.00									
	Total Assets			Total Liabilities			Total Equity			
	$ 249,831.00			$ 1,500.00			$ 248,331.00			

Fg. 10

If you've got a calculator at the ready, then you should be able to create a trial balance for the Donut Shop. Do this now on a separate sheet of paper. If you're struggling, let's walk through the process:

1. Identify the total balance of each account in play. Lucky for you, the cash account has its balance posted on the bottom left corner of the spreadsheet: $244,831.

2. The equipment account only has one entry, so its balance remains at $25,000.

3. The Accounts Payable (Maverick's) balance is $750*2 or $1,500.

4. The Accrued Payroll account has a credit entry of $630 and a debit entry for the same amount. Its total balance, therefore, is $0.

5. Your expense account has five debit entries, totaling to a negative value of $7,220.00.

6. The revenue account has two credit entries, totaling to $8,751.

7. The Owner's Capital account has one credit entry of $250,000.

8. Finally, the Owner's Withdrawal account has one debit entry, a negative value of $3,200.

9. The next step is to list all of your debit and credit totals. This listing is made easier using a table:

Account Name	Debit Balance	Credit Balance
Cash	$ 224,831	
Equipment	$ 25,000	
AP (Maverick's)		$ 1,500
Accrued Payroll	$ 0	$ 0
Expense	$ 7,220	
Revenue		$ 8,751
Owner's Capital		$ 250,000
Owner's Withdrawal	$ 3,200	
TOTALS	$ 260,251	$ 260,251

Your trial balance reveals that your total debit balance is equal to your total credit balance.

When the credit and debit account totals do not match, you have an accounting problem that must be investigated. There is a specific process to investigate erroneous trial balances with maximum efficiency:

- **Step 1** : Check the arithmetic. Hopefully the reason the totals don't equal out is because someone simply punched in an incorrect number into his or her calculator when adding the two columns together.

- **Step 2** : If you've still got an error after checking your arithmetic, then go back to the account ledgers that were used (in this case, it was just a spreadsheet) to determine the balance for each account. If you didn't record the correct balance, then that is likely the cause of your error.

- **Step 3** : Check to see if a debit entry was listed as a credit (or credit entry listed as a debit). This obviously throws off your numbers. In fact, if this is your only error, then the difference between your disparate balances equals twice the value of the erroneously entered account balance. For example, in your trial balance above, if you'd listed the Owner's Withdrawal account ($3,200) as a credit balance rather than a debit balance, then your debit/credit totals would have been: $257,051/$263,451, a difference of $6,400, or ($3,200*2).

- **Step 4** : If you're still unable to reconcile your balances, then you need to bite the bullet and go through each ledger and re-compute its account balance.

- **Step 5** : Check to make sure that all journal entries made were posted properly to their ledgers.

- **Step 6** : Verify that each original journal entry contained an equal amount credited and an equal amount debited.

Note : When the trial balances equal out, it's a good thing, but it is not an iron-clad guarantee that no accounting errors have been made. The trial balance still equals out when equal credit and debit entries are made to the wrong accounts. Trial balances also equal out if a single erroneous number is used to determine both a debit and a credit entry, and since double-entry accounting involves making entries in pairs, this type of error is always possible. Double-checking is always a good idea!

Now that you know how to prepare trial balances, you are ready to begin the all-important discussion of *financial statements*.

| 6 |

Financial Statements

If accounting is the language of business, then *financial statements* are the bridge between those who are fluent in the accounting language and those who merely have a cursory understanding of it. You don't have to be an accountant to make extraordinary use of financial statements. CFOs are hired (and paid well) to produce these statements so that executives, owners, managers, and shareholders can make intelligent decisions based on the information that the statements contain. It is through the crafting and application of financial statements that accountants set themselves apart from bookkeepers, who are but mere mortals.

External & Internal Users

Individuals who use financial statements can be divided into two main groups, external users and internal users. *External users* can include lenders who may be considering whether or not they want to give your small business a loan. An auditor working for the IRS who thinks that you may be skimping on your taxes is also an "external user." Shareholders of a company are external users, too, as are civic or community groups that are considering working with your business in some charitable capacity (usually culminating in a healthy tax break for your business). An external user may also come in the form of a new prospective partner for your business, whether it's an individual who wants to buy in or another business that wants to merge. These parties need to see financial statements.

Internal users are the people within the business who use financial statements, such as you, the owner, as well as your managers, officers, sales staff, and internal auditors.

Types of Financial Statements

Here's a breakdown of the four most basic and widely used types of financial statements: income statements (also known as Profit/ Loss), statement of owner's equity, balance sheet, and statement of cash flow. Balance sheets—such as a beginning balance sheet and an ending balance sheet—are pertinent to a <u>particular point in time</u>. They are usually stamped with a date, as opposed to a date range. Income statements, statements of owner's equity, and statements of cash flow all refer to a <u>time period</u>, such as a calendar year, fiscal year, or week.

For the purposes of this book, the following statements are technically **unadjusted statements**, since they are not presented with all of the common adjustments usually included, such as depreciation. The purpose of this chapter is to give a basic understanding of the main financial statements, what information they include, and how they're used.

An **income statement** focuses on the company's revenues and expenses over a period of time, as well as the business's net income or net loss over that same period. Sales professionals in your business use the balance sheet to track the business's sales revenues and ensure that they're meeting their targets. The trial balance, with its clear listing of revenues and expenses, informs the income statement. Revenues are often broken down into multiple different subcategories for different revenue types, and expenses are likewise broken into different categories, such as rent, utilities, and salaries. Total revenue and total expense are both shown. Total expense is subtracted from total revenue to provide a net income amount for the period. This **net income** amount is used in the statement of owner's equity.

A **statement of owner equity** shows how equity in the business changes over time. The statement of owner's equity is generally divided into two separate sections, plus and less, with plus showing increases in owner equity and minus showing decreases. The "plus" section contains the owner's capital investments into the business added to the business's net income for the period. It helps to have your various financial reports defined according to the same period of time. If your income statement is for the fiscal year 2015, then your statement of owner's equity should adhere to that same time period, as you need to carry your business's net income from the former report and add it to the plus section in the latter. The "less" section of the owner's equity report contains all the withdrawals the owner has made. Subtract the less from the plus, and you've got the current owner's equity, also known as the "end of period capital balance." This balance is used to configure the balance sheet.

Note : The end of period capital balance for one period is always the beginning of period or "opening" capital balance for the next period. So, if the owner's equity report for the 2015 fiscal year has an end of period capital balance of $250,700, then the report for the next year has this same number as the beginning capital balance. This way, the owner's equity statements stay fluid and traceable from period to period. The owner's equity report needs some adjustments if there are additional owners, as the net income of the business is not divided between the owners in proportion to their ownership percentages.

The **balance sheet** details a business's financial situation in a given period of time. It is a breakdown of the business's assets, liabilities, and equity. Balance sheets are generally issued at the end of a significant period, such as the end of the fiscal year, or at the end of a quarter. Balance sheets, sometimes, stay true to the left/right theme of the fundamental accounting formula, loosely itemizing and listing the business's assets on the left, while loosely itemizing and listing its liabilities and equity on the right (including the end of period capital balance as reported in the statement of owner's equity). This left/right presentation of the balance sheet is known as the **account form**. Another format, called the **report form**, lists all of the assets on top and the liabilities and equity on the bottom. The total assets and total sum of liabilities and equity is shown at the bottom of the balance sheet, and, as you know by now, these sums should be equal to one another.

Republic of the Philippines
MUNICIPALITY OF SAN NARCISO ZAMBALES

STATEMENT OF CASH FLOWS
GENERAL FUND
For the Period Ended March 31, 2011

Cash Flow from Operation Activities :

Cash Inflows:		
Collection of taxes	3,445,953.57	
Internal Revenue Allotments	11,166,537.00	
Interest Income	0.00	
Other Receipts	328,724.34	
Total Cash Inflows:		*14,941,214.91*
Cash Outflows:		
Payments -		
To Suppliers/Creditors	4,083,166.16	
To Employees	4,693,555.19	
Total Cash Outflows:		*8,776,721.35*
Net Cash from Operating Activities		6,164,493.56
Cash Flows from Investing Activities :		
Cash Inflows:		
Receipts for Purchase of PPE	0.00	
Total Cash Inflows:		*0.00*
Cash Outflows:		
Purchase of Property, Plant & Equipment	0.00	
Total Cash Outflows:		*0.00*
Net Cash from Operating Activities		0.00
Cash Flow from Financing Activities :		
Cash Inflows:		
Proceeds from Loans	0.00	
Total Cash Inflows:		*0.00*
Cash Outflows:		
Purchase of Loans	0.00	
Total Cash Outflows:		*0.00*
Net Cash from Financing Activities		0.00
Cash Provided by (Used in) Operating, Investing, and Financing Activities		6,164,493.56
Add: Cash Balance, December 31, 2010		31,817,424.62
Cash Balance, March 31, 2011		37,981,918.18

Fg. 11

The *statement of cash flow* clarifies the inflow and outflow of cash over a specific period of time and is used to ensure that the company has enough cash-on-hand to expediently pay its liabilities without having so much cash sitting around that it becomes a fraud risk. The statement of cash flow is generally broken down into cash flows from operating activities, cash flows from investing activities, and cash flows from financing activities. Operating activities include the operation of the business, receiving revenues, paying employees, and paying for supplies and other expenses. Investing activities track the cash that's been invested in equipment, real estate, or other major assets. Financing activities refer to cash coming in through capital investments, either by the owner or by an outside party. Owner's withdrawals of cash from the business are also tracked under financing activities. The statement of cash flow below, from a government municipality in the Philippines, shows how the statement is broken down into its component parts.

Even though the example statement of cash flow (*Fg. 11*) refers to a rather large entity, cash flow management is exceptionally important to small businesses. Findlaw.com reports that hiccups in cash flow are one of the most frequent problems that entrepreneurs encounter. Part of the problem here is that your small business may find itself at times with more cash-on-hand than actual income, meaning your net income as reported on the income statement may be less than your cash balance for the same period. As a result, business owners sometimes use up cash faster than their business can generate it, leading over time to financial insolvency.

There are a multitude of viewable sample images available on the Internet of all the statements covered in this chapter. Unfortunately, most of them are not licensed for commercial use, so we can't include them in this text. To look at examples, do a Google image search for the terms below.

- Income statement
- Statement of owner's equity
- Balance sheet
- Statement of cash flow

| 7 |

Budgeting for Your Business

"It's time to prepare a budget." Those words instill fear in even the most fiscally- responsible individuals. Budgeting is a daunting proposition for both households and businesses, but every good financial steward should consider it, whether you are managing a home and family or a small corporation, partnership, or sole proprietorship.

Budgeting is all about being prepared for what is coming next. It pertains to the future and where you hope to take your business. Budgeting also provides a look at your business as it stands NOW and gives you the opportunity not only to take stock of what is happening at the present but to take control of what you want to happen in the year (or years) to come.

Not everyone budgets. You may know that from personal experience. How many of us tend to flounder a bit in our early years especially, overspending when we get that first big job or when we get married and blend two incomes? No doubt, if that was you, you may have found yourself in a bit of trouble and pondered the fact that perhaps you should have devised a budget first, before you overspent. But *should* everyone budget, especially businesses?

Not necessarily, says John Tracy in his book, *Accounting for Dummies*. "Keep in mind that budgeting costs time and money," he points out. "The business manager should put budgeting to the classic technique: the cost versus benefit test."

Even if you decide formal budgeting is not right for your business, he adds, you shouldn't summarily dismiss it. Tracy notes that certain techniques used in budgeting might be very useful to a particular business even if it chooses not to go all the way with very elaborate budgeting.

Why Budget?

Every business should have a strategy and a list of financial goals. If it doesn't, who's to say where it's going and how it will get there? Often, a stagnant business is a boring and frustrating business and one that tends to eventually give up the proverbial ghost.

However, when you choose to budget, you are setting *specific* goals and planning for *specific* ways to reach them. All of a sudden, you've instituted "drive" not only in yourself – the owner – but also in your managers and employees, who now have a collective goal as well. You may already have some of these goals in your head and perhaps have for some time, but budgeting forces you to put them down on paper (or in a spreadsheet) where they can be reviewed and adjusted. With a budget, you have clear destination points.

Budgeting also allows for better control. While a budget is NOT meant to stifle spending or quash ideas, it can indeed serve a management control function. Control doesn't mean looking over the shoulders of your managers or employees to be sure that they're following the budget to the number, but it does mean giving them a guide to help them achieve financial goals and objectives and reach certain benchmarks during a particular time period, particularly when you've divided the budget into smaller increments, like monthly or quarterly. This is also why it's a good idea to involve your managers – if you have any – in the budgeting process and perhaps award them in some way when goals are reached.

In regards to new businesses, drafting a proposed budget is helpful when trying to raise capital. Your potential investors want to be convinced that you have a sound strategy and realistic plans in place in order to make profits. No one wants to invest in a business that doesn't know where it is going and how it might arrive at Point X. So, a "budget forecast" is an especially important part of any new or emerging company's business plan.

Budgeting Basics

Budgeting sounds like a big deal, and it can get complicated if you let it. But it really is as simple as keeping good records and reviewing them to form a forecast and goals for the future.

For established businesses, start by developing sound models of profit, cash flow, and financial condition. A model is exactly what the word suggests – a plan or blueprint of how things work. Models don't need to involve a lot of accounting – that is, mathematical calculations – but should be analytical.

Analyzing and budgeting for the year ahead starts with these models:

A Profit Report or Budgeted Income Statement

A profit analysis model includes variable as well as fixed expenses, like sales volume and the profit margin per unit sold or service performed. All of the items on the budgeted income statement must be improved in order to enhance profit and reach goals for the following year. Hence, once the report is created, it needs to be reviewed to determine how these improvements will happen.

Budgeted Balance Sheet

This should include the "key connections and ratios between sales revenue and expenses and their corresponding assets and liabilities," Tracy explains. This information is essential for budgeting cash flow in the time period for which you are budgeting.

Budgeted Statement of Cash Flows

This is a super-important aspect of budgeting. It helps the owner or manager to predict changes in assets and liabilities for the coming year, which determines cash flow. It also informs the owner's or manager's decisions regarding any capital expenditures for the upcoming budgeted time period. This includes how much new capital the owner may have to contribute and how much new capital will be raised from debt. It also includes a policy regarding any cash distributions made from profits.

If this seems complicated, just remember that the reports you use for budgeting (and others you may use along the way) give you a solid look at the financial condition of the business. Your accountant may have ideas to help you assemble these, or you can use budgeting software programs to assist you. With these schematics in place, you can make better decisions and more effective plans.

When Not to Budget

Though the reasons for budgeting are many, some businesses needn't take the leap into the world of planning for the future in such detail. For example, companies that aren't planning any huge changes (additions or discontinuities) in the near future can probably get along without spending time and money to draft a budget. So, if you think the next year of your business will be a lot like the current one, budgeting is a waste of your time.

Some businesses may also be in an environment that makes it difficult to predict exactly what will happen in the future, making budgeting an exercise in futility.

Others lack personnel with the expertise needed to draw up the kinds of budget blueprints described in this chapter. They also may not have the resources to invest in expensive budgeting software or to hire an accountant.

Budget experts suggest, however, that if formal budgeting is not an option, the mere fact that you're keeping good internal accounting reports goes a long way in planning for the future. Owners and managers should make a habit of sitting down to review profit reports, balance sheets, cash flow statements, and other account reports on a regular basis, using them to make more "informal" future plans.

Budgeting Software for Consideration

Below is a list of some of the best-selling budgeting software for small to medium businesses.

Budget Maestro

Centgage offers this software designed to help with budgeting, forecasting, financial consolidation, performance analysis and reporting processes. Reviewers say it works for a wide variety of industries, is easy to use and, when combined with the company's Link Maestro and Analytics Maestro, can not only design a budget but also produce the necessary financial reports needed to do it.

Plan Guru

This one includes features that assist with budgeting, forecasting, and even performance review. Small businesses like its simple setup, its import features, and its 20 different forecasting methods, which are customizable to different kinds of businesses. However, it was built for accountants, so it may be a little complicated for those who don't have extensive accounting experience.

Pulse Cash Flow Management

Created by small business owners for small businesses, Pulse provides a simple way for owners and managers to understand their current cash flow and make decisions to improve it in the future.

It's a good combination of accounting software and forecasting tools but nothing too overwhelming for smaller businesses.

Quicken Home & Business

Quicken has developed a fine reputation over the years, and this particular software has so many potential applications. Great for sole proprietorships and S corporations, it offers tools for budgeting monthly expenses and forecasting for the upcoming year. It's inexpensive and doesn't require a lot of time to learn how to use it.

Palo Alto Software Business Plan Pro

This planning and budgeting software is designed specifically for those launching new businesses. It offers tools to help develop a business plan and budget that can be presented to bankers and other potential investors. Professional-looking charts, graphs, and reports can be printed at the touch of a button, and the company is especially known for its excellent support team. It's cheap, too, but mostly meant for beginners in the realm of budgeting and forecasting.

| 8 |
Fraud & Ethics in Accounting

Not every business will be hit with fraud, but it does happen. Sometimes small businesses are more apt to experience it, especially if only one person is handling the books. That's why a system of checks and balances is always a wise idea. Other steps can also be taken to reduce fraud.

Ethics and fraud prevention are critical aspects of accounting. An accountant's responsibilities require an exceptional degree of ethical decision making. When you handle a company's finances, you're in a position of high abuse potential. Nonetheless, most accountants respect their position and do their job without stepping over the line, but if something doesn't seem right financially, it's time to do some investigating.

But while accountants may be in a position to succumb to fraud, they are also in a position to sniff out and prevent fraud in their companies.

When an accountant suspects fraud in the company, he is expected to follow this three-step process:

1. The accountant must use his own sense of ethics to identify a potentially troubling issue. Maybe there are abnormal journal entries that don't conform to the usual rhythm of business.

2. Once an ethical concern is identified, the accountant must consider all the positive and negative repercussions of taking action to investigate the concern. Is the money of such a small amount that it would only truly be problematic were it to turn

into a recurring anomaly? If so, then maybe the best course of action is to hang back for a while before bringing the issue to the attention of the company owner or manager.

3. After all of the pros and cons have been weighed, it's time to make the best decision for your business. Remember, in accounting, smart is ethical and vice versa.

It's a well-documented fact that most theft comes from within an organization rather than outside of it. If someone steals a significant quantity of inventory from your jewelry store in the middle of the night, the odds say that an employee is probably the guilty culprit as opposed to a burglar. And what's true for burglary is, of course, true for embezzlement.

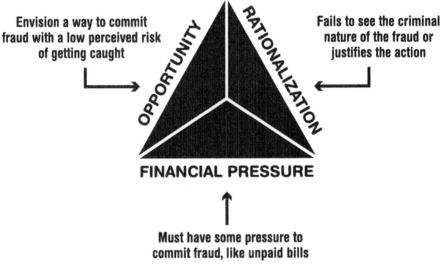

Envision a way to commit fraud with a low perceived risk of getting caught

RATIONALIZATION

Fails to see the criminal nature of the fraud or justifies the action

OPPORTUNITY

FINANCIAL PRESSURE

Must have some pressure to commit fraud, like unpaid bills

Fg. 12

The fraud triangle, pictured above in *Fg. 12* , has been used for decades to assess and respond to internal fraud issues. As a small business owner, you should be on the watch for the three main factors depicted in the triangle:

Opportunity

There will always be some individuals who are tempted to steal. It doesn't matter whether they've been with you for just a few months or for many years. Some will indeed scope out opportunities to defraud the business. You may never understand why, or, with some investigation, the reasons they thought they could get away with this may become clear. *However,* if this employee is merely seeing the opportunity without feeling the financial pressure or generating a rationalization to execute the nefarious scheme, then she may prove valuable in ensuring that the business never succumbs to one of the plots she envisions. Good accounting involves beating the embezzler to the punch. Figure out the scheme before the schemer and prevent it, and you'll be in a better position to intercept an embezzler in his or her tracks. As was mentioned previously in this text, small businesses don't have the same remedies available to them as larger businesses when it comes to fraud prevention. Larger businesses intentionally diffuse bookkeeping and accounting responsibilities across a large pool of employees and departments to foster a system of checks and balances that inherently minimizes fraud. For a smaller business, you, the owner, are the most important deterrent, so be mindful of opportunities for fraud within your business.

Rationalization

Rationalization can either refer to an inability to see something as criminal or the willful and personal decision to see something as justified. Most individuals don't begin work in a company planning to defraud the owner at the first opportunity. The will to commit fraud is built up over time, often resulting from perceived slights or abuses of the employee by the owner or a manager. A rationalization may occur if an employee feels that he's not being adequately compensated, so dipping into the company's petty cash account every odd Thursday isn't necessarily unethical behavior in his eyes.

Note : It's important to reemphasize again that fraud cannot be prevented in a business, only minimized. Take, for example, the employee who feels he's under-compensated. Though it would be great if you could pay everyone exactly what he thinks is fair, that's not the reality. In reality, most small business owners try to pay people what they perceive to be a fair market rate for the work being provided. The fact that some employees, at some point in time, may feel that they're being underpaid and use this as a rationale for fraud is unavoidable. Accept that fraud can only be minimized, not wholly prevented.

Financial Pressure

The third segment of the fraud triangle is Financial Pressure. It refers to an employee's personal financial circumstances, bills that need to be paid, a sick relative, a skyrocketing gambling debt. When a person is facing enormous financial pressure, he's more likely to succumb to committing fraud.

As a small business owner you should assess the three main factors in the fraud triangle in tandem to evaluate the risk of fraud at your business. When all three factors are present, then there is a high likelihood that the employee will attempt to defraud your business. Your focus should always be on making it more difficult for fraud to occur in your company. It's generally a lot easier and less expensive to prevent fraud from occurring than it is to detect fraud in action.

Here are some of the actions you can take to minimize the risk of fraud in your business:

- Use locks and passwords on sensitive records, allow people to access sensitive financial information on a need-to-know basis.

- Most fraud comes from maintaining large quantities of cash and other liquid assets on a work site. Minimize fraud by minimizing the amount of cash and other liquid inventory items available to employees, especially employees who may be more likely to attempt to defraud the business.

- Be aware of being defrauded from the outside through the use of fraudulent checks. Banks these days don't even check signatures anymore, but rely instead on numeric codes and other controls. Keep close banking relationships. Your business should have a primary contact point at the bank you use, someone who is familiar with you and your business and can vouch for you if something goes wrong.

Last, but definitely not least, you have to police yourself, the small business owner. It may seem very tempting to write off certain personal expenses as business expenses, but doing so can make you guilty of fraud. If you plan a vacation to Bermuda, and you take a couple of business phone calls while soaking up the sun, don't think you suddenly have the option to write off your vacation expenses as business expenses. It's very important that the identity of the business entity be maintained and its boundaries well defined. The next chapter goes into a little more depth on defining the business entity with a discussion of GAAP, the Generally Accepted Accounting Principles.

| 9 |
The GAAP

The US Securities and Exchange Commission instituted the **GAAP** system of rules to make sure accounting methods are somewhat uniform throughout the country. Imagine if IRS auditors were required to spend valuable time and energy on the taxpayer's dime learning the unique, quirky accounting methods of every business. The point of GAAP is to advance a set of clear, fair, and optimal principles that all businesses are expected to follow. If you think about it, standardization is good for accountants as well, as it ensures that if you know how to conduct your accounting in accordance with GAAP standards, you're imminently hirable throughout the country. GAAP also protects stockholders and stock traders who need a clear way of comparing various businesses side by side. Can you imagine how difficult it would be to try to make a smart investment decision when you have to sludge your way through and make judgments about several disparate financial records?

Smaller businesses don't need to worry about highly specific GAAP principles, but should adhere closely to the broader principles governing good accounting practice. The owner of a smaller business should understand what's commonly referred to as "The House of GAAP," which is built on four principles (the colonnades which thrust the house upwards prominently), four assumptions (the base of the house upon which the colonnades/principles rest), and the two constraints (the foundation of the house, which, were it not stable and amenable, would cast the entire structure asunder).

The Four Principles

1. The Measurement Principle

This is also called "The Cost Principle." When you buy a tractor for your farming business for which the sticker price is $13,000 but you're able to negotiate the price down to $12,000, you *must always* record the price that you paid, or the exact amount of credit you were issued to make the purchase. You would record $12,000, and under no circumstances would you record $13,000. This is known as the measurement principle. At the heart of this principle is verifiability. The cash amount used to make a purchase or the amount received in exchange for a good or a service is a lot easier to verify than the sticker price of a John Deere industrial tractor at Jimmy Red's Tractor Lot on May 10th 2013.

Note : The measurement principle does, of course, allow for adjustments to the value of property purchased in accordance with accepted standards for depreciation.

2. The Revenue Recognition Principle

With this principle, the GAAP clearly identifies itself as an ***accrual-based accounting*** methodology rather than a ***cash-based*** methodology. The revenue recognition principle holds that revenue is recognized (accounted for) at the point at which it is earned, not necessarily at the point at which is paid. Imagine you're the owner of a mental health professional conglomerate. Collectively you've had 150 hours of client sessions and you've sent out $120,000 in invoices, but only $60,000 has been paid. According to GAAP, you should still report $120,000 in assets.

Note : Technically speaking, you'd report the $60,000 that's been paid as revenue and the remaining $60,000 as an accounts receivable asset. Assuming, however, that some of your clients are simply never going to pay you for your services, which is a factor many businesses must face, you'd be able to depreciate the value of your $60,000 by crediting it for the amount you're not likely to ever receive,

> *then debiting your equity in a specialized expense account that you can call "non-payment." From that point forward, you'll always be able to assess how much your company's net income is suffering due to clients that don't pay.*

Simply put, according to the revenue recognition principle, the proceeds from selling products and services need not be in cash but can also take other forms, such as a promise to pay (credit). A business's revenues are thus measured both by the quantity of cash it receives and the value of any other assets that are obtained through the sale of goods and services.

3. The Expense Recognition Principle

This one is pretty straightforward. The expense recognition principle holds that a business is always required to report expenses alongside revenue. As you learned in Chapter 2 of this book, both expense and revenue accounts are equity accounts, and, as you found out in Chapter 4, revenues minus expenses generate a business's net income. So, readers of this book should already have a good understanding of the importance of tracking expenses.

4. The Full Disclosure Principle

According to the full disclosure principle, businesses must always report in detail items on a financial report that would impact the users of the financial report. For example, if you were about to receive a loan from a bank on behalf of your business, and you knew that your business was about to be subjected to a serious rent increase, then you would need to report that detail on your financial statement to let the prospective lender know that you're soon to be facing higher costs. Full disclosure items are often added to the end of the financial report in the form of footnotes.

The Four Accounting Assumptions

1. The Going Concern Assumption

This assumption holds that a business is going to continue to operate and will not be sold or closed. For example, if you're reporting equipment as an asset, then you must report the cost of the equipment rather than the liquidation value that would only be relevant if you were selling the equipment.

2. The Monetary Unit Assumption

This assumption holds that accounting records are always reported using monetary values such as dollars. Depending on the country in which the business operates, different monetary values may be used. It's also, at times, necessary for reports to be issued in different versions for different currencies.

3. Business Entity Assumption

This assumption repeats the discussion at the close of the previous chapter—the importance of treating the business entity as an entity of itself, as opposed to merely an extension of the business owner. A lot of small business owners get into hot water over violating this assumption, thinking they can blur the line between themselves and their businesses. The fact that owners of sole-proprietorships and partnerships are subject to *pass-through taxation*—which means that, for tax purposes, the business and the individual are treated essentially as a single entity— gives some business owners the requisite rationalization to think they can get away with not keeping clear boundaries between what's business related and what's not.

4. Time Period Assumption

This assumption holds that a company's function may be divided into specific time periods—months, years, fiscal years—and that reports can be devised to intelligently comment upon this periodic financial activity.

Now you've arrived at the foundation of the "House of GAAP", the accounting constraints:

1. Materiality Constraint

Have you ever watched a courtroom drama and heard an attorney say, "It's immaterial!" The materiality constraint says that businesses need only record and report information that has the potential to influence the decisions of a reasonable person. In other words, if you buy an extra pen at the supply store before going into a meeting and you neglect to save the receipt or file and report it as an expense, then you're probably not going to end up in jail. The pen was immaterial.

2. The Cost Benefit Constraint

This simple constraint holds that disclosures are only necessary when their benefits outweigh the cost of producing them. In other words, the cost of providing financial statements is measured against the benefits garnered by the users of that information. If it is determined that this information is negligible, then it can be left out of the financial statements.

It is sometimes difficult for a small business to quantify the benefits associated with said information, which makes this constraint rather confusing. In larger companies, it is usually easier to determine whether investors or creditors will benefit from having access to certain information.

| 10 |
Sizing Up The Software

As a person interested in at least having a basic grasp of accounting, one of the things you're probably wondering is: *Well, doesn't accounting software like Quickbooks pretty much do all of my accounting work for me?*

The truth is that Quickbooks and other accounting software do a great job taking care of a lot of the math and making it easier to set up and organize your accounts, but it's no substitute for basic accounting principles. A lot of small business owners find it a lot simpler just to keep four filing cabinets – one for assets, liabilities, revenue/expense, and owner capital/withdrawals—as a way to accomplish their accounting requirements rather than be too terribly reliant on software. Software should be used to expedite the journal entries, posting, and the formation of reports, but you'll also need to keep some tangible records, such as receipts, in your filing system.

According to Linda Pinson, the author of *Keeping the Books: Basic Recordkeeping and Accounting for the Successful Small Business*, "One of the mistakes businesses make when they buy accounting software is in believing that they don't need to know anything at all about financial accounting because the software will just take care of it for you."

Furthermore, a lot of the fundamental principles in this book, including charts of accounts, debit/credit, and others, are used in accounting software. You're going to get more mileage out of your software if you have a solid understanding of basic accounting principles before the download.

That said, accounting software can benefit both you and your accountant or bookkeeper when used properly and consistently, making it a wise purchase for many small business owners.

When it's time to choose the best software for your business, recognize that there are many options. According to Mike Budiac, "It's real important to get this right. In a lot of cases, it can make the difference between businesses that are profitable versus not profitable." Mr. Budiac runs a website that helps people locate accounting software that fits their businesses. His website FindAccountingSoftware.com offers a survey that directs users to the ideal software for their businesses. There's also a toll-free number that you can dial for some independent advice.

Here are some of the main factors that you should consider when selecting a piece of accounting software that's right for your business:

Computer Literacy

How computer literate is the business owner or the employee who's going to be in charge of keeping the books and utilizing the software?

Using "The Cloud"

Are you comfortable running your accounting software in the Cloud? A lot of noteworthy names in accounting software, such as Quickbooks, Netbooks, NetSuite, and Clarity Accounting, have launched online-only versions of their products. If you're comfortable running all of your accounting through a secure remote server, then this might be the option for you, as it's generally cheaper.

How Much Can Your Business Afford To Spend?

Many of the basic-package accounting software options have a pretty reasonable entry-level price point, but once you start getting into industry-specific, specialized programs, that price can spike dramatically.

What Type of Business Do You Operate?

A lot of different accounting programs have specific versions or add-on modules that accommodate certain business types. Remember, if your business manufactures children's toys, it's going to have accounting needs that are very different from those of a physician's conglomerate.

What Type of Business Do You Operate?

What are the limits of your business's hardware capacity? Some of these accounting programs are real bruisers when it comes to sucking up computing resources. Check with your IT department to get an idea of what's possible with your current configurations.

Additional Functionality

What additional functionality does the business want included with its accounting software program? Does it benefit from an add-on point-of-sale program or a customer relationship management add-on? Is the business primarily concerned with using the software to manage payroll?

Another option you have when selecting software is to temporarily hire an accountant to help advise you on this decision. Meanwhile, this temporary CFO may also be able to introduce you to a handful of tips and tricks to get your financial records in better shape. One company that offers part-time CFO help is called B2B CFO (www.B2Bcfo.com).

It would also be prudent to nose around and find out what businesses similar to yours are using for accounting software. Read reviews in magazines and online. And finally, when you make your selection, make sure that you're given a risk-free trial period. If it doesn't work, send it back and try something else.

How do you know when it's time to invest in accounting software?

1. **Your business is just beginning.** If you're just starting to cut your teeth as an entrepreneur, then it's best to get your accounting software set up sooner rather than later. If you try to keep your accounting in spreadsheets or on handwritten ledgers, you'll find that it's incredibly grating and time consuming to relay all the records over into your accounting software. If you start by using the software, then your data is imminently more portable.

2. **Your business is beginning to grow.** Though it's entirely possible for a very small business to opt not to use accounting software at all, electing instead to use the four filing cabinet system explained earlier in this book, if your business is beginning to grow, then you'll probably want to opt for software-assisted rather than manual accounting. In the modern day, there's a point at which the business's records become too voluminous for manual accounting to be the most efficient accounting method.

3. **Are you trying to streamline functions?** If you're in a business in which a lot of time gets wasted performing tasks that can be streamlined, then accounting software may be just what the doctor (or the accountant) ordered. Accounting software gives you the opportunity to hybridize various critical business functions, such as payroll, taxes, and financial reporting. Use your software judiciously, and it could add miles to your productivity.

4.   **Got legal concerns?** A lot of small business owners turn to accounting software when they're looking to address a legal problem-point within their businesses. While good accounting software can definitely clarify your records, when you're facing an audit, and you're worried that you might be breaking the law, or unsure on whether or not you owe a tax penalty, then you're better off consulting with a real licensed accountant, not just a software program.

5.   **Do you need mobile access?** Unfortunately, you can't carry around physical filing cabinets in your pockets. Most accounting software gives users the option of accessing their data and generating reports from their mobile phones. If this is something that's important to you, then be sure to try out your chosen software's mobile capabilities during that all-important trial period.

Choosing the right (or any) software is an incredibly broad topic and heavily dependent on the type and size of your business. The questions and speculation points in this chapter are designed to get you thinking in the right direction. At some point, however, you have to turn to the market at large and make the best decision for your business.

Good luck!

conclusion

If you feel you have a good understanding of all the material in this book, then you've already done a lot of the heavy lifting when it comes to learning accounting. You understand the difference between debits and credits. You understand how accounts are organized and how the data contained in accounts are presented to various users. You grasp the importance of ethics in accounting and how those individuals (including accountants) who work around a business's books can be both susceptible to fraud and in a unique position to prevent it.

This goal of this book was to get you from a point of knowing virtually nothing about formal accounting, to having a practical, useful handle on how accounting works, how it's standardized, and why it's important to so many businesses. When it comes to expanding your knowledge on accounting, there are volumes upon volumes of books and materials you can study.

If you'd like to learn a little more about some of the basic accounting theories, principles, and methods, then you can find another beginner-friendly text in John A. Tracy's, *Accounting for Dummies*.

Another book, published by Kaplan, is directed at small business owners seeking to pick up some accounting basics. The book is written by Linda Pinson and it's called: *Keeping the Books: Basic Recordkeeping and Accounting for the Successful Small Business*.

Another great way to learn more is by taking an intro to accounting course at your local community college or university.

bonus quiz

Match the Account Described to the Account Type

The following quiz describes several different accounts. Your job is to match the account with its appropriate account category—Asset, Liability, Revenue, Expense, Owner Capital, or Owner Withdrawal.

Case 1 : A Real Estate Conglomerate –

The following questions pertain to the accounting used at a real estate conglomerate, "The Sampson Group," which hires Coast Property Management to oversee its many rental properties.

1. What type of account does the Sampson Group use to report rental payments from tenants?

2. When the Sampson Group first formed, they raised capital by issuing 5-year and 10-year bonds. For accounting purposes these bonds are considered _____.

3. The Sampson Group purchased a vehicle in the company's name so the owners could write off gas mileage for business trips. The vehicle is insured through Progressive insurance. What type of account is used to keep track of vehicle insurance?

4. The apartments in one of the Sampson Group's properties experienced a wave of vandalism. As a result, the Gold Coast Property Management Company quickly purchased and set up a new security system with additional lighting and security

cameras. Gold Coast Property Management will not bill the Sampson Group until the following month. Until the bill is paid, Sampson will keep the cost of the new security set up in what type of account?

Case 2 : Sail Away Boat Tours –

The following questions pertain to the accounts of a private touring company that operates in the Florida Keys.

5. Sail Away Boat Tours has a fleet of twelve different boats that cost, on average, $35,000 each. Over the course of five years the value of these boats depreciates, making them, as assets, less valuable. If the boats are listed as "assets," and, as assets, are credited when the boats decrease in value, which account gets debited when the boats depreciate in value?

6. After being in operation for 20 years, the original owners of Sail Away Boat Tours decide to sell the entire company to a mysterious multi-millionaire who has plans for rapidly expanding the business. After he purchases the business, he immediately adds one million dollars to its cash coffers using his own money. Under what account type would this influx of capital be recorded?

7. The proper licensure is obtained and Sail Away Boat Tours becomes authorized to sell beer and liquor on the boat during the tours. The company managers order $5,000 worth of alcohol and keep it stored. Under what account type would the alcohol reserves be categorized?

8. Once the mysterious multimillionaire expands the company, it operates a fleet of 60 boats throughout the Florida Keys and

throughout all of south Florida. The company management decides that they're going to offer a money-back guarantee to customers to get them to try out the tour. Any customer dissatisfied with his or her experience on Sail Away Boat Tours will be fully refunded the entire amount of the ticket price. The executives estimate that about .5% of customers are going to redeem this offer and get a refund, and the total estimated value of lost revenue for the current fiscal year is $17,897. Under which account would this amount be recorded?

Answer Key on the following page...

answer key

1. Revenue
2. Liability
3. Expense
4. Liability
5. Expense
6. Owner Capital
7. Assets
8. Liability*

* This is a tricky one, but if a company is large, you have to estimate the cost for any warranties or guarantees that you issue to the public. Then you must estimate how much these warranties/guarantees will cost the business. Since these obligations represent the eventuality of value leaving the business, they are considered properly as liabilities.

glossary

The Accounting Equation-
See "Fundamental
Accounting Formula."

Accounts-
A record of the increases and
decreases in the worth of a specific
business asset, liability, equity
value, revenue, or expense.

Account Form-
A particular type of balance sheet
formatted so that all asset accounts
are listed on the right, and equity and
liability accounts are listed on the left.

Accounts Payable-
A type of business liability that
increases as the business acquires goods
and services before paying for them.

Accrual-based Accounting-
Bases transactions on the outflow and
inflow of actual goods and services. Not
as common in small businesses as is its
counterpart (cash-based accounting)
For example, cash received by a
business for services not yet performed
does not constitute revenue, but does
constitute a liability. Once the good
is provided or service performed,
then the liability is transferred out
of liability and into revenue.

Assets-
Resources owned by the business
that provide or promise value
for the business, such as cash,
property, equipment, investments,
and accounts receivable.

Balance Sheet-
A listing of values (in dollars) of
a business's assets, liabilities, and
equity, recorded at a specific date.

Cash-based Accounting-
A method of accounting that, though
common for small businesses, is not
the method recognized by the certain
standardized accounting institutions
of custom, such as GAAP. In cash
accounting, transactions are defined
by the inward and outward flow
of real cash, not necessarily by the
exchange of actual goods and services
(see accrual-based accounting).

CFO-
Stands for Chief Financial Officer. This
is an executive position in a business,
usually given to an accountant. Broadly
speaking, the CFO is in charge of
an organization's financial affairs.
In smaller businesses, especially, the
main role of the CFO is to ensure
that the business remains profitable.

Chart of Accounts-
A complete listing of a business's
accounts, grouped under the
main headers of assets, liabilities,
revenue, expenses, owner's equity
and owner's withdrawals. The chart
of accounts includes a listing of
the account numbers assigned
to each individual account.

Credit-
A type of accounting entry that decreases the value of an asset account, increases the amount owed on a liability account, and increases equity accounts, such as expenses, revenue, and owner capital and withdrawals.

Debit-
A type of accounting entry that increases the value of an asset account, lowers the amount owed on a liability account, and decreases equity accounts, such as expenses, revenue, and owner capital and withdrawals. Chapter 2 of this text is devoted to explaining how credits and debits are used in accounting.

Double-Entry Accounting-
Refers to a powerful, nearly-universally-used accounting methodology whereby every internal and external accounting transaction must be recorded in two different accounts, once as a credit and once as a debit.

Equity-
After a business's assets have been used to account for all of its liabilities, what's remaining is known as equity. Equity is what the business's owner(s) are entitled to keep.

External Users-
In accounting, external users refer to parties outside the business who may need to access and interpret the business's financial data. For a small business, a bank considering giving a loan to the business is an example of an external user, as the bank wants to assess the business's financial health before determining whether to issue a loan.

Financial Statements-
Reports that interpret a business's financial data in a way that's useful to business decision makers. Examples of financial statements include income statements, owner's equity statements, cash flow statements, and balance sheets.

Fundamental Accounting Formula-
Assets = Liabilities + Equity.
This may also be referred to simply as "the accounting equation." This equation is the bedrock for a multitude of important accounting principles.

GAAP-
Generally Accepted Accounting Principles, a system of guidelines aimed at making financial information relevant, reliable, and comparable. GAAP guidelines in the United States are set by the Securities and Exchange Commission.

General Ledger-
See entry for "Ledger."

Income Statement-
Also known as a Profit/Loss Statement, this financial statement subtracts the business's expenses from its revenues to show how a business's net profit is calculated.

Internal Users-
Internal users refer to the parties within a business who use financial reporting data. Owners, managers, sales managers, budget planners, advisors, and accountants all qualify as internal users.

Journal Entry-
A record that notes a business transaction that affects the balance of a business's accounts. Journal entries are used to update account ledgers.

Ledgers-
A general ledger is a record containing all of the accounts that a business uses. There are also account specific ledgers, which are used to track individual accounts.

Liabilities-
Claims on a business's assets, such as debts, accounts payable, salaries payable, legal fees payable and anything else that obliges the business to remit value in exchange for value received at an earlier time.

Net Income-
Refers to the amount the business earns as calculated by revenues minus expenses. Also known as "income," "profit," or "earnings."

Notes Payable-
A type of liability account characterized by an obligation in writing that guarantees the business will pay a lender a certain sum by a certain date.

Posting-
The process of moving information from a journal entry to a ledger. Posting involves identifying all the accounts that the journal entry affects, finding the ledgers for these accounts, and updating them according to the changes specified on the journal entry. Today, most posting is achieved by computerized automation.

Posting Reference-
Also commonly referred to as PR. Posting References are usually tracked in journal entries and on ledgers as a way to allow users to trace transactions.

Report Form-
A type of balance sheet on which accounts are listed vertically, beginning with asset accounts at the top, followed by liability and equity accounts.

Source Documents-
Bills, sales tickets, receipts, register reports, bank account statements—these documents are used to acquire information about the projected value of a business's accounts.

Statement of Cash Flow-
A common financial statement that tracks cash as it comes in (receipts) and departs (payments). The statement of cash flow is broken down into operating cash flow, investment-related cash flow, and financing cash flow.

Statement of Owner Equity-
A financial statement that records the changes in owner equity over a certain period of time. Owner equity changes can include owner investment and net income (increases) and withdrawals and net losses (decreases).

Trial Balance-
A snapshot listing of all accounts and their balances at a specific point in time. The trial balance totals all debit balances with all credit balances to ensure that they're equal to one another.

Unadjusted Balance-
A listing of organized accounts that have been prepared without making standard accounting adjustments.

about clydebank

We are a multi-media publishing company that provides reliable, high-quality and easily accessible information to a global customer base. Developed out of the need for beginner-friendly content that is accessible across multiple formats, we deliver reliable, up-to-date, high-quality information through our multiple product offerings.

Through our strategic partnerships with some of the world's largest retailers, we are able to simplify the learning process for customers around the world, providing them with an authoritative source of information for the subjects that matter to them. Our end-user focused philosophy puts the satisfaction of our customers at the forefront of our mission. We are committed to creating multi-media products that allow our customers to learn what they want, when they want and how they want.

ClydeBank Business is a division of the multimedia-publishing firm ClydeBank Media LLC. ClydeBank Media's goal is to provide affordable, accessible information to a global market through different forms of media such as eBooks, paperback books and audio books. Company divisions are based on subject matter, each consisting of a dedicated team of researchers, writers, editors and designers.

For more information, please visit us at :
www.clydebankmedia.com
or contact *info@clydebankmedia.com*

Your world, simplified.

notes

REMEMBER TO DOWNLOAD YOUR FREE DIGITAL ASSETS!

Visit the URL below to access your free Digital Asset files that are included with the purchase of this book.

☑ Summaries   ☑ White Papers
☑ Cheat Sheets   ☑ Charts & Graphs
☑ Articles   ☑ Reference Materials

DOWNLOAD YOURS HERE:

www.clydebankmedia.com/accounting-assets

ClydeBank Media is a Proud Sponsor of

AdoptAClassroom.org

AdoptAClassroom.org empowers teachers by providing the classroom supplies and materials needed to help their students learn and succeed. As an award-winning 501(c)(3), AdoptAClassroom.org makes it easy for individual donors and corporate sponsors to donate funds to K-12 classrooms in public, private and charter schools throughout the U.S.

On average, teachers spend $600 of their own money each year to equip their classrooms – 20% of teachers spend more than $1000 annually. Since 1998 AdoptAClassroom.org has raised more than $30 million and benefited more than 4.25 million students. AdoptAClassroom.org holds a 4-star rating from Charity Navigator.

TO LEARN MORE, VISIT ADOPTACLASSROOM.ORG

CPSIA information can be obtained
at www.ICGtesting.com
Printed in the USA
BVOW06*1506251117

500177BV00026B/137/P

9 781945 051456